W9-AVA-725

PowerKiDS
Readers
SAFARI ANIMALS

HIPPOS

Clara Reade

PowerKiDS
press.
New York

For Mark Zhang

Published in 2013 by The Rosen Publishing Group, Inc.
29 East 21st Street, New York, NY 10010

First Edition

Editor: Amelie von Zumbusch
Book Design: Greg Tucker

Photo Credits: Cover, pp. 5, 7, 9, 11, 13, 15, 19, 21, 23 Shutterstock.com; p. 17 Anup Shah/The Image Bank/Getty Images.

Library of Congress Cataloging-in-Publication Data

Reade, Clara.
Hippos / by Clara Reade. — 1st ed.
    p. cm. — (Powerkids readers: safari animals)
Includes index.
ISBN 978-1-4488-7392-0 (library binding) — ISBN 978-1-4488-7472-9 (pbk.) —
ISBN 978-1-4488-7545-0 (6-pack)
1. Hippopotamus—Juvenile literature. I. Title.
QL737.U57R43 2013
599.63'5—dc23

2011048013

Manufactured in the United States of America

CPSIA Compliance Information: Batch #CS12PK: For Further Information contact Rosen Publishing, New York, New York at 1-800-237-9932

CONTENTS

Hippos live in Africa.

4

They always live near water.

6

1

Hippos spend the day in the water.

9

This keeps them cool.

10

At night, they feed on land.

13

They eat grass.

14

15

A baby hippo is a **calf**.

Some calves are born underwater.

A group of hippos is a **pod**.

21

People hunt hippos.

22

WORDS TO KNOW

calf

hippo

pod

INDEX

WEBSITES

Due to the changing nature of Internet links, PowerKids Press has developed an online list of websites related to the subject of this book. This site is updated regularly. Please use this link to access the list:
www.powerkidslinks.com/pkrs/hippos/

24